MW01600366

Whales for Kids

Explore the Fascinating World of the Ocean Giant and Learn Everything You Need to Know About Them

Table of Contents

Introduction

Whale, hello there! Welcome to the world of whales!

Hello there! Source: Designed by Freepik.
https://www.freepik.com/free-vector/realistic-magical-dreams-
background_31682074.htm#fromView=search&page=1&position=
0&uuid=2976adf6-f350-4f40-934e-285722a88113&query=whale

Have you ever wondered what life is really like under the sea for your favorite gentle giants?

If you're interested in learning all about whales, how they live, and how they spend their days, but haven't found easy-to-understand information explained in a fun, simple way, you've come to the right place!

Whether you know a little about these deep-diving flipper friends or are brand new to the world of whales, step off the plank and dive into an ocean of knowledge.

Here, you will learn the most un-beluga-ble facts about whales. So, grab your snorkel and get ready to dive underwater!

This book provides everything you need to become an expert on whales, from what these sea creatures eat and how they talk to what adventures they get up to underwater.

So what's in the book?:

- The world of whales
- The types of whales
- Crazy whale quirks and flips
- Whale songs and calls
- The differences between whales and other ocean giants
- How to become a whale hero

It's important for children to learn about whales, the whale rescue team, and how to help them.

Packed with FACTS and FUN, *Whales Facts for Kids* has thrilling pages about:

- The biggest mammals on earth!
- The different temperatures whales live in, from the icy cold Arctic to the hottest coasts.
- The different sizes of whales – the largest being as long as 3 school buses, like the blue whale!

- Whale food, and these midnight munchers' favorite snacks!
- The acrobatic ocean dwellers, like the humpback whale.

In this book, you will:

- Meet the two types of whales, from the ones with teeth to the ones without – baleen whales.
- Learn about a day in the life of a baby whale (tiny giant).
- Discover whale language and how they communicate through songs, clicks, and whistles!
- Learn about their habitats and which ones like a sunny home by coral reefs and which like an ice-berg paradise.
- Discover the heroic efforts of the whale savers and how you can help, too!
- Learn about whale talents and tricks!

Whale Facts for Kids isn't just another boring book that just dumps information on you. This book will have you clicking, whistling, and singing whale tunes!

So, are you ready to become the ultimate ocean explorer?

Keep reading to find all the answers you're looking for, and start your journey big, like a loud, flipper slap on the water's surface.

Have a whale of a time!

Chapter 1 – Welcome to the World of Whales

In this chapter, you will learn all about the different types of whales.

What Makes a Whale?

Since they have fins and live underwater just like other fish, you might think whales are fish, too. But they're mammals just like us! Whales live in the ocean, but they have a lot in common with you and your pets on land!

Take a look at what makes a whale!

They're Big

It may be obvious that whales can grow pretty big. Just how big? Well, they are called the largest animal on planet Earth for a reason. Some whales, like the blue whale, can grow to be bigger than a T-Rex!

They're Intelligent

Whales are smart! In a way, they're like humans. They talk to each other, sing along with one another, and even play games together.

They Breathe Air

Like dogs and dolphins, whales breathe in air. Like us, they don't breathe underwater. They hold their breath until they come up to the surface for air and breathe in and out through a blowhole.

They Are Warm-Blooded

Another thing whales have in common with people is that they're warm-blooded. Even though the ocean can get very cold, whales stay warm.

Whales vs. Fish: What's the Big Deal?

Even though whales and fish both live underwater and are excellent swimmers, there are many differences between them.

- **Whales Are Mammals – Fish Are Fish**

Like cats and dogs, whales are mammals – fish are not.

- **Whales Breathe Air – Fish Breathe Underwater**

Whales have lungs, like us, and blowholes on top of their heads. They need to come up for air. Fish have gills instead of lungs and can breathe underwater.

- **Fish Lay Eggs – Whales Give Birth to Babies**

Whales have babies, called calves, and feed them milk just like human moms feed their babies. Baby fish hatch out of eggs that the mommy fish lay, similar to birds.

- **Fish are Cold-Blooded**

As you learned, whales are warm like people. Fish are cold because their body temperature changes to suit living in the ocean.

- **Fish Swim with Their Bodies – Whales Use Their Tails**

Whales wag their tails up and down to swim in the ocean. Fish wiggle their bodies from side to side through the water.

Meet the Whale Family

The Different Whale Species

1. Toothed Whales
2. Baleen Whales

Toothed whales have teeth, so they eat things like fish and squid.

Instead of teeth, baleen whales have combs, like the one you use for your hair. They only eat tiny animals like krill.

Types of Toothed Whales

1.   Beluga Whale

*Source:
https://commons.wikimedia.org/wiki/File:Oceanogr%C3%A0fic_2
9102004.jpg*

They live in the Arctic and love to sing songs.

2.   Narwhal Whale

*Source:
https://commons.wikimedia.org/wiki/File:Narwhal_(PSF).png*

Known as the "unicorn of the sea" because they have a big tooth on top of their head like a horn.

3. Sperm Whale

Source:
https://commons.wikimedia.org/wiki/File:Mother_and_baby_spe rm_whale.jpg

Moby Dick was a sperm whale. These whales are super smart – they have the largest brains.

4. Orca Whale

Source: https://www.pexels.com/photo/close-up-shot-of-an-orca-at- the-seaworld-9355603/

This whale is also known as the killer whale, but it is actually a dolphin. They're very intelligent and quick swimmers.

5. Dolphins and Porpoises

Source: https://www.pexels.com/photo/dolphin-jumping-out-of-water-11342081/

Believe it or not, these are whales, too! They are called small-toothed whales.

Types of Baleen Whales

1. Blue Whale

Source: https://commons.wikimedia.org/wiki/File:Blue-Whale-0009.jpg

This is the biggest animal on the planet.

2.   Grey Whale

Source: https://www.pexels.com/photo/gray-whale-3329230/

These can swim for thousands of miles.

3.   Humpback Whale

Source: https://www.pexels.com/photo/close-up-shot-of-a-humpback-whale-6134290/

The best singers in the ocean.

4. Right Whale

Sadly, they got their name from hunters naming them the right whales to hunt.

5. Fin Whale

These are the second largest whales after the blue whale and are called the "greyhounds of the sea."

6.   Minke Whale

Source:
https://commons.wikimedia.org/wiki/File:LMazzuca_Fin_Whale.j
pg

This is the smallest baleen whale, but it is still bigger than most animals.

How Calves are Born and Raised

Baby whales or calves take almost a year to grow in their mother's belly. They can be as long as a car by the time they are born.

Calves stay by their mother's side until they are strong and smart enough to survive on their own. Their moms teach them how to get food, swim, and stay safe.

Moms, Dads, and Pods

A whale family has a dad, mom, and calves (brothers and sisters). Mommy whales are strong and protective when caring for their calves. The dads don't usually stay with the mom and baby whales. They go off with the other whales or pods. The mom and baby whales join the pods when the calf is old enough.

Pods are a group of whales – friends or family. Some have dozens of members, while others are just a group of 4 or 5. Whales who are part of a pod travel together, play games, and keep each other safe

Growing Up

Calves start their lives coming out of their mothers, right by the tail, so they can quickly swim up to the surface to breathe. The baby drinks its mother's milk to help it grow big and strong.

The mother whale teaches her babies to talk, sing, swim quickly, find food, and hold their breath underwater for a long time. Like human children, calves learn through playing. They roll around in the water, splash around with their tales and take big jumps. Playing helps them get stronger and smarter. When they're older (and bigger), they join a pod and make friends.

Fun Fact

- **Whales Have Belly Buttons**

Just like you, whales have belly buttons because mammals grow in their mothers' bellies and are fed by a cord in the belly button known as the umbilical cord.

- **Blowholes Are Noses**

Blowholes are a whale's nose!

Whales breathe in and out through the hole on top of their head instead of a mouth. They help whales hold their breath for a long time and can make a big, tall splash as air comes out. Some whales, like the blue whale, have two blowholes!

Chapter 2 – The Giants of the Sea

Learn all about the size and weight of the loudest and heaviest animals on the planet. There's a reason they're called the giants of the sea!

Whale Size Showdown

From smallest to largest, this list shows you which whale wins the size showdown!

Dwarf Sperm Whale

The smallest whale is only 9 feet in length – the same as a very large dog or a a kayak.

The dwarf sperm whale is a quiet little soul and belongs to the toothed whale species.

Minke Whale

The second smallest is not that small. It can reach up to 35 feet long. However, it is the smallest baleen whale.

Female minkes are slightly bigger than male whales.

Gray Whale

These whales can be between 45 to 49 feet. These baleen whales don't have teeth. Instead, their brittle mouth filters food from the ocean.

They also have a hump of small, sharp bumps instead of a dorsal fin.

Right Whale

These whales are about 45 to 52 feet when fully grown but some can reach up to 60. These lovely baleen whales feed on tiny crustaceans, using their mouths like the sieve you have in your kitchen.

Humpback Whale

Your favorite singing whale can grow as long as 52 feet.

The humpback is another baleen whale on this list and are mostly black in color with white patches on their fins, bellies, and on parts of their tails.

Bowhead Whale

Source:
*https://commons.wikimedia.org/wiki/File:A_bowhead_whale_bre
aches_off_the_coast_of_western_Sea_of_Okhotsk_by_Olga_Shp
ak,_Marine_Mammal_Council,_IEE_RAS.jpg*

This baleen whale reaches about 59 to 60 feet in length and can jump really high out of the water.

Bowhead whales can live a long time, much longer than most animals.

Fin Whale

These whales are the second largest and can be between 72 to 90 feet, but most of the time, they reach up to 85.

These baleen whales get the zoomies, making them super fast swimmers.

Blue Whale

The largest animal on earth can grow up to 90 to 100 feet – that's the size of a basketball court! They are larger than the biggest dinosaur and their weight is equal to 33 elephants.

Weighty Facts (How Much Whales, Eat, Poop, and Weigh)

Whales Eat a Lot!

Whales must eat a lot for their large sizes.

The blue whale can eat 4 to 16 tons of krill (shrimp-like creatures) a day. That is equal to a human eating between 8000 to 65,000 burgers! Each whale meal is the same size as a car. Imagine eating a car-sized plate of food three times a day!

Whales eat a lot of krill! Source:
https://www.flickr.com/photos/onms/27026776971

Baleen whales eat small fish, krill, and other shrimp-like creatures. Toothed whales catch fish and squid, and because they have teeth, they can go for larger animals like seals.

A sperm whale will eat about 1 ton of squid a day. So, their daily meals are about the size of a small car. Having teeth gives them an advantage when hunting.

Bowheads have the biggest mouth, so they trap a lot of food through the baleen (the bristle teeth-like comb they have to filter food).

Whales Poop... A lot!

All that food has to come out sometime, and when whales need to go, they can poop 50 gallons at once. That's about 200 liters of water.

A whale's poop is fluffy and large. It even floats up to the surface. Tiny ocean plants feed on it, and fish feed on the plants, so whales keep the ocean healthy and every living thing in it fed.

Weight of Whales

As you know, the blue whale is huge! It weighs up to 200 tons. Imagine carrying 2,500 people or 33 elephants – that's the weight of the biggest whale.

However, even the smallest whales are big! Baby sperm whale calves still weigh at least 600 pounds when they're born. That means they can weigh the size of a fire hydrant or even up to a full-sized pool table.

Whales Breaking Records (Longest, Heaviest, and Loudest)

It's no wonder that if there were a contest for the longest, heaviest, and loudest animal, whales would win everytime time!

- ## Longest Whale

Balaenoptera musculus size comparison

The blue whale holds the record of the longest whale. It is over 100 feet long – the size of a small airplane. It even has the largest organs, with its tongue weighing the same as an elephant, and its heart the size of a small car!

- **Fastest Whale**

The fastest whale is the orca with a speed of swimming 35 miles per hour, especially when searching for fish to eat!

The orca is the fastest! Source: https://www.pexels.com/photo/orca-in-sea-24778635/

Fin whales are the fastest baleen whale. They have a high speed of 30 miles per hour when swimming away from danger.

Whales may be big, but their bodies are designed to swim fast in water. Their tail wags help them move quickly, and their strength gives them an advantage over their prey. They're living proof that being big doesn't necessarily mean you have to be slow!

- **Heaviest Whale**

The blue whale wins again!

It should be no surprise that the largest whale is also the heaviest. The blue whale is as heavy as 30 school buses – between 200,000 and 400,000 pounds.

- **Loudest Whale**

The sperm whale wins the loudest animal award! It is on record for making sounds up to 230 decibels – that's louder than a jet engine!

Blue whales can be loud, too! Their heartbeat can be heard from 2 miles away. Imagine your heartbeat being heard by people a block away from you!

Tiny Giants

Baby whales, also called calves, are only small to other whales. They're still bigger than other animals. Sperm whales have big babies that can grow to 13 feet – the size of a small truck.

Orca whale babies can be 8 feet long and 350 pounds when they're born. That's the height of a door or dining table. They weigh the same as a piano or large refrigerator.

The Life of a Baby Whale

Baby whales are born knowing how to swim and whistle. Their mothers whistle when they're in her belly, so they can recognize the sounds as soon as they come out!

A baby whale starts their day swimming up to the surface with their mother to take their first breath of air. They always stay close to their mothers for safety.

Whale calves drink milk from their moms until they are 1 or 2 years old. They drink a lot, too – about 100 gallons of milk. That's like you drinking 2 large bottles! As they get older, they copy their mother and switch to eating tiny sea creatures like krill.

Mommy whales teach their calves everything about swimming and getting strong to keep her babies safe.

The baby whale. Source: Designed by catalyststuff on Freepik. https://www.freepik.com/free-vector/cute-whale-swimming-cartoon-vector-icon-illustration-animal-nature-icon-isolated-flat-vector_221771453.htm#fromView=search&page=1&position=11&uuid=302ab13b-a3d3-496e-bf5c-6e73317df6fd&query=baby+whale

Baby whales spend much of their time playing. They love to play by splashing around and jumping out of the water. They also spin in circles to get stronger. Plus, it's fun!

They learn important things through playing and swimming, like how to follow their pods and stay safe from sharks.

At night, baby whales need to rest. They float next to their moms and the entire pod swims together slowly. When calves fall asleep, only half of their brain sleeps. The other half stays awake to breathe and swim.

Chapter 3 – Whale Talk and Ocean Chatter

Whales are more talkative than you think! They communicate with each other through pulsed calls, clicks, and whistles.

They call and whistle mostly when they're playing or during social activities. Clicks are used to give directions while traveling the ocean. They let each other know what's going on around them to keep the pod safe from danger.

Whale Songs and Clicks

Whale Songs

Whale songs are very special sounds. Whales sing to send messages and grab the attention of other pod members.

Humpback whales are the most talkative and are well-known for their singing. Their beautiful songs can be heard all around the water, and whales may repeat their favorites over and over again for hours!

In whale language, singing is communication. They sing to chat with friends and family and even belt out love songs to get the attention of a mate.

While whales love to sing, they don't have vocal cords like humans. So, their sounds come from their blowholes. Air is pushed through these holes to make all the sounds they need and ensure other whales can hear them from far away.

The humpback males sometimes sing the same tune as other males to bond. They basically start their own musical band! They even change their tunes every now and then, so the songs never sound alike.

Whale Clicks

While humpbacks love their vocal runs, other whales stick to making clicking sounds. Sperm whales always click to communicate their needs. Clicks are basically chit-chatting for whales. These are short sounds that bounce off objects in the water, so they can be heard for miles.

Whales click to talk to their friends and share important information, such as their location, so other whales can find them or be warned about danger nearby.

Some whales, like the humpback, are singers. Others, such as the sperm whale, are more chatty. Just like people, whales have different accents. Think of it like another nationality. There are songs and clicks for different whale types as if they have their own language.

How Whales Communicate Underwater

Pulsed Calls

Whale communication also includes calls. Orca whales (killer whales) use pulsed calls the most. These can sound like bird squawks, squeaks, or screams. But they're not in pain – it's just how they talk. They are a loud bunch!

Whistles

Whistles are quite high-pitched sounds, similar to human whistles. These are how whales greet each other. A whistle can mean "Hello!"

Orcas are quite friendly, so they use many whistles, calls, and clicks to talk to each other. Within the orca family, there are many different accents. Orca pods develop their own secret language to communicate with each other.

Clicks

Clicks can also be a way for whales to say hi to each other, but they are most often used to find food and warn each other of their surroundings.

Clicks are used often by the loudest whales, sperm whales. Sounds travel farther in water than they do on land, so a sperm whale's clicks can be heard for hundreds of miles. Clicks are magical, too. They help whales see in the dark when they bounce off objects or other animals like squids.

Moans

Some whale types, like baleen whales, don't sing tunes. They make low-sounding moans instead. Blue whales and grey whales always seem chill! They like to have a chat while swimming with friends and family.

However, just because they sound calmer does not mean their voices aren't heard. A blue whale's moan can travel as far as 1,000 miles away. Imagine yourself being able to give your friends a shout-out from another country! That's how powerful a whale's moan is.

Singing for Love, Maps, and Friends

Whales sing for many reasons. Sometimes, it's for love and friendship. Other times, they sing out directions, like how people would draw a map for others to find them.

Songs are very important to certain whales because they use melodies and sounds to communicate with their group and navigate the ocean. They consider singing a job. Some of these jobs can be as long as a 20-minute concert!

Singing for Love

Whales, like the humpback, sing love songs to find a partner. Male whales may sing to show their strength and impress female whales. The females choose their mates based on which one carried out the best tune!

Whales sing songs to find a partner. Source: Designed by catalyststuff on Freepik. https://www.freepik.com/free-vector/cute-couple-whale-with-love-cartoon-vector-icon-illustration-animal-love-icon-concept-isolated_23654560.htm#fromView=search&page=1&position=1&uid=5bd8be5d-4a90-4aa6-b7bc-f75ce237094d&query=whale+love

This is very common among humpbacks because they learn to sing these social calls from as young as a month old. Most of the time, it is the male humpbacks that sing. Female humpbacks prefer to just listen.

Singing to Draw a Map

Songs can be how whales make a map to help others navigate the waters. They do it so all members of the pod find their way back to each other.

Orca whales sing to ask other whales about their location. This helps them find out exactly where they are in the ocean, especially if they're on a long journey to somewhere new.

Songs are a whale's way to map out the sea. Whales follow these tunes and track how far they've traveled across the ocean and how much further they have to go.

Singing for Friendship

Whales don't just sing for love. They sing to their friends, too. They talk to them through melodies as a way to call out to them, especially if their friends are far away.

Whales listen to each other's songs. It helps them know the location of their families and pods. It keeps them together and helps them stay in touch when they're at a distance. The ocean is a big place, and it's easy to get lost, so whales stay safe by letting others know where they are and how to find them.

Whale songs are used during social interactions and encourage other whales to come out and play. They help whales learn about their environment and can even be a way for whales to communicate their needs.

Whales can inform their families, friends, and pods of their emotions, like whether they are happy or scared. This way, others can find them, so they all stay safe together.

Baleen whales use singing for this purpose the most. They share information this way to identify where their group is and help others identify them. Their songs change over time because pod members add their own unique styles.

Whale songs are designed in a way that follows a pattern, making it easy for other whales to learn their languages.

Some whales, like humpbacks, have a wide range. That means they can sing really high and low! These mammals can also sing for hours. The longest record of a whale song was 30 minutes long, and the longest singing session that humans know about was apparently 22 hours!

Chapter 4: Super Smart Sea Creatures

These giant water dwellers don't just talk together. They can speak in different accents and languages. Are they smarter than you, though? Can they sit down for a test or solve a puzzle? Do they have street smarts? Do they have schools that teach them new things every day?

Whales are super smart! Source: Designed by catalyststuff on Freepik. https://www.freepik.com/free-vector/cute-whale-employee-holding-bag-cartoon-vector-icon-illustration-animal-business-icon-isolated-flat_259674706.htm#fromView=search&page=1&position=34&uuid=93807661-e962-45e9-9a1b-04e66c92a7e9&query=smart+whale+

Well, if you're looking for answers to these questions, you've come to the right place.

Whale Brains Are Huge... But Are They Smart?

Whales are the biggest mammals on Earth today, so it kind of makes sense that their brains are also the biggest. Does big equal smartest, though? The answer is no.

You may think that because the blue whale is the biggest whale out there, it means they have the biggest brain. Well, that's not true.

The biggest brain belongs to the sperm whale. Sperm whales have the largest brain among all the animals in the world. However, they are not the smartest in their species.

There is something called the cerebrum, which is the part of the brain that controls movement, learning, and the information gathered from the senses. This cerebrum is smaller in the sperm whale's brain compared to the blue whale. That makes the blue whale smarter.

But still, how smart are they?

Whales have a built-in sonar in their brains. They use something called "*echolocation*" to scan the area around them, checking for prey, other whales, and sometimes sending messages to each other.

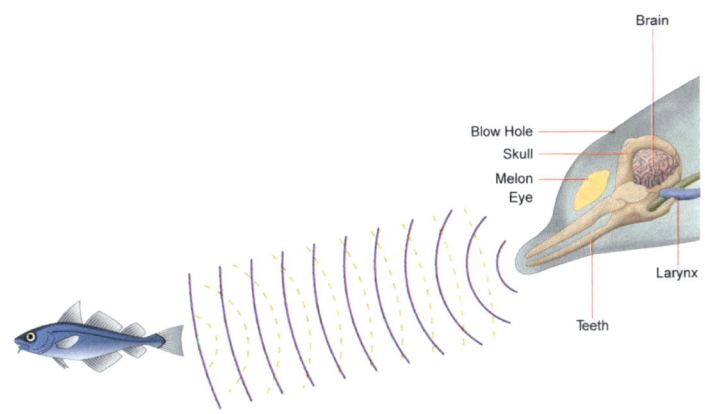

Whale using echolocation. Source:
https://commons.wikimedia.org/wiki/File:Toothed_Whale_Echolo
cation.png

Whales can also recognize and remember one another. They can work in groups and solve problems, like tricking hunters, evading capture, and organizing their own hunts.

Fun Fact

- Sperm whale brains can weigh up to 20 pounds. If you're wondering how big that is, your brain is about 3 pounds! That means 1 whale brain equals almost 7 human brains.

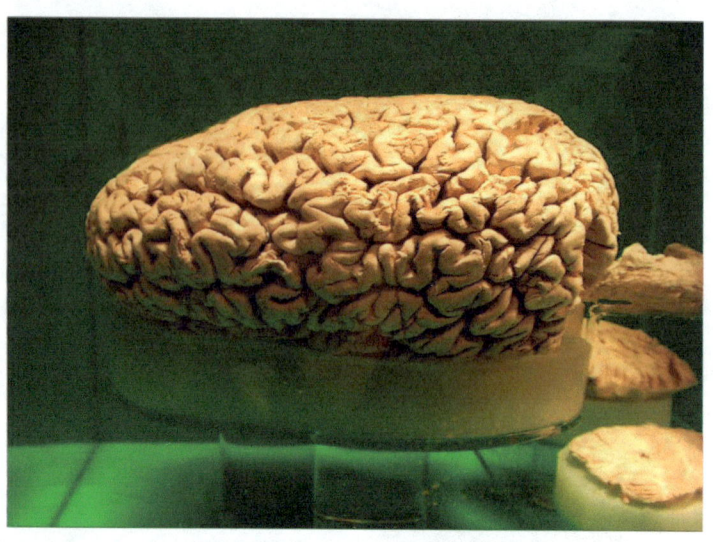

Sperm whale brain. Source:
https://commons.wikimedia.org/wiki/File:Preserved_sperm_whal
e_brain.jpg

Families, Friendships, and Whale Culture

Did you know that part of being intelligent is the ability to make friends and have family relationships? Everyone used to think that only people could share feelings and understand them. Everyone was wrong.

Like humans, whales have nerve cells in their brains called ***spindle neurons***. These cells help them socialize, build a community together, and have emotional connections, just like people do with their family and friends.

Sperm whales can have best friends just like you. The neurons in their brains allow them to pick favorites they like to hang out with and talk to more than others. Also, just like people, whales can feel sad when they lose a family member.

A family of whales can consist of 4 to 20 members, cooperating together, and helping each other with different responsibilities. For example, some babysit, while others eat.

The smaller whales learn from the older ones. Older whales, whether mothers or grandmothers, pass information down to the younger ones and teach them by example. They teach them about migration routes and behaviors through social interaction. This is called culture. If a whale is helped as a calf, it helps out the family more when it grows up.

Fun Fact

- Sperm Whales can build bonds so strong that they sometimes use the toilet at the same time.

How Baby Whales Learn from Their Pods

In sperm whale pods, mothers get help from the rest of the family.

When the little calves are born, they babble like human babies, and it can take them up to two years to learn how to talk. To help them, the older whales use baby talk to teach them how to make conversations.

Baby whales learn by talking to each other. Source: https://www.flickr.com/photos/rokal/8044441786/

Baby whales can recognize their mother's voices even before being born. After birth, when talking to their mothers, calves "whisper" so other predators don't hear them. From a young age, the pod teaches the babies how to use different sounds to socialize together and with other whale clans.

Orcas, for example, start to learn from their pods right after they're born. They watch and copy how the older members hunt, protect themselves and each other, share techniques, and talk to one another.

In a pod, the mother is the main character in the baby's life. They travel closely together while she teaches them how to communicate and hunt. Unlike other animals, mother whales can stick around their young even after they become adults. This ensures that the calves always have knowledgeable members around the pod to provide help if needed.

Playtime in the Ocean

Being playful usually means you're clever, and whales are expert players. The champions of playtime among the whales are dolphins. They enjoy playing together and with humans.

Whales are expert players! Source: Designed by Freepik.
https://www.freepik.com/free-vector/hand-drawn-wild-animals-
illustration_26411787.htm#fromView=search&page=2&position=6
&uuid=48d30275-f2c5-4404-b10e-
993f92594b8a&query=whales+playing

You've probably seen them racing boats, chasing each other, jumping out of water, skidding on the water using their tails, back flipping, and all kinds of fun shenanigans. Imagine surfing a wave near the shore, looking to the side, and seeing a dolphin riding it with you. Yes! That could definitely happen.

Dolphins can even use seashells and plants as toys. Sometimes, they have playdates with other whales, like the humpbacks. Dolphins were seen using the humpback's nose as a slide. The whales would pick them up and splash them over and over.

Some orcas even fetch things and deliver them to boats as a game, which is similar to playing fetch with a dog.

Fun Fact

- Dolphins sometimes use other animals as toys, like turtles. They take turns throwing them to each other like a ball (poor little fella).

Signs of Whale Emotions

Whales don't use facial expressions and limb movements to show how they feel like humans and other animals. Scientists think they use sounds.

In 1999, some of those scientists thought they heard a dolphin laugh during a play session with its buddies.

Some scientists believe that whales also mourn the dead. Some mothers carry the deceased babies for days and even weeks after they pass. When a whale is in distress or trapped in a net, the pod usually comes together to help it, which means they feel empathy for each other.

Fun Fact

- Whales can show emotions to humans, too. Sometimes, they guide people to shore when they are lost.

Chapter 5: Whales on the Move

If you're wondering how and where to spot a whale with your very own eyes, you're in the right place.

Whales of all kinds love to travel. They have their secret routes in the ocean. These journeys they take are called migrations, and they happen during the different seasons of the year. These trips caught the attention of some really smart people, like scientists and marine researchers, so they started paying attention and building maps to predict where and when the whales will be.

Whale GPS

Whales have their own GPS. Source: Designed by Freepik.
https://www.freepik.com/free-vector/environmental-concept-
paper-
style_6849445.htm#fromView=search&page=1&position=9&uuid=
af9324d2-3f58-4061-9783-d6b35eac8e25&query=whales+gps

In the summer, whales travel all the way to the polar regions, where they can find all

kinds of their favorite foods. They eat krill, small fish, and plankton to store energy in the form of blubber.

In the winter, whales travel towards warmer areas to build families and give birth to their baby calves.

But how exactly do they find their way in the water when humans sometimes lose their way in the streets with GPS?

Some scientists believe that whales have their own GPS within their bodies. One of the theories is that whales use the magnetic fields of the Earth to guide them on their journey.

- Another theory suggests that they use echolocation. This means that the songs and sounds they make bounce off other objects in the ocean, giving them an idea of what's around them and where they are.

- A third group of researchers thinks that whales use navigation techniques similar to old sailors, like the direction of the water currents, the temperature of the water, and the position of the sun, to know where they are.

So, where can you spot whales? These aquatic giants are seen a lot along the North American west coast.

For example, grey whales show up in the south between November and January, and in the North in March and April. During those times, the mothers travel with the babies near the shoreline.

Humpback whales also make an appearance during their annual trip in the spring and summer along the whale trail.

Orcas tend to be more unpredictable than others. They like surprises and could pop up at any time.

Dolphins and seals like to make an all-year-round appearance, especially near the shores.

Seals like to make an all year round appearance. Source: https://www.pexels.com/photo/grey-sea-lion-2524194/

A long time ago, in the 1990s, people started to realize that tour operators spend a lot more time in the ocean than researchers do.

To make it easier to find the whales and dolphins for tourists, they started recording the places and times when whales were seen using something called data sheets. Boat captains were trained on how to take down the details of these sightings.

Nowadays, there are apps that people can download to record when they see a whale or a dolphin. These apps then create a pattern with the history and predict when the next whale will show. It then puts the information it gets from the users on a real-time map that you can easily follow.

Scientists also use underwater listening devices, called hydrophones. These devices record the sounds that nearby whales make, and then pinpoint where they are on a map. These maps show the location where the whale was detected, whether they are sure of the detection or not, the season of the year, and other details to help find them.

Around the World in 80 Waves

Whales exist in almost all parts of the world. You can see them in shallow and deep waters and cold and warm currents, roaming between the two poles.

Whales are excellent swimmers. They don't mind traveling for thousands of miles just to get to a warmer climate or find food.

Not all whales are easy to track. For example, Bryde's whales are usually easy to pinpoint. They tend to stay in tropical areas like the northern part of the Gulf of California. In contrast, scientists can't track where the southern right whale travels to feed in the winter. However, they do know that they roam near South America, South Africa, and Australia in the summer to breed.

Since dolphins enjoy staying near the shores, they are much easier to track down. They migrate when the currents get cold, but not as far as whales do.

Humpbacks swim all the way from Antarctica to Australia (Queensland) to deliver their babies and build their families.

Southern right whales enjoy the southern coasts of Australia, while the blue whales can be seen in the Bonney Upwelling, filling their bellies with krill.

Whale Highway Rules

Remember, when you're on a boat in the ocean, you're practically in the whales' home. This means sailors and boat owners need to respect the rules around the homeowners.

A lot of the time, whales face the dangers of vessel traffic in the water, which often happens when their migration routes pass near crowded ports and shipping lanes.

While whales are considered the biggest mammals on earth, they are not always clearly visible to boats, which puts them at risk of being injured by the vessel.

Around 20,000 whales are killed every year by boats, while others are hurt by propellers and endure tail and fin flukes.

The IWC (International Whaling Commission) has yet to find a solution to protect the gentle giants. For the time being, they try to move boats away from the migration routes of the whales and their natural habitats. When that's not possible, boats are advised to slow down and be mindful of their surroundings so as not to harm or injure the animals.

For tour boats observing whales, there are other rules that need to be followed:

- Boats should move slowly when approaching whales and should stay at least 60 meters away. If the whale seems distressed, they have to move back.

- The boat shouldn't block the whale's movements or cut it off.

- Boats can't use sonar to locate the whales.

- They can only move parallel to the whale at a speed that doesn't exceed 4 knots an hour (around 4 miles).

- If a whale comes close to the boat, it must be placed in a neutral position.
- There can't be more than two boats within 300 meters of a whale.

What not to do:
- You can't feed the whales
- Dive or swim with them
- Stop the boat in their path
- Move between a mother and a baby
- Approach them from the front or back

Baby on Board

While they are called babies, a newborn blue whale can reach 25 feet long. That's as big as a small swimming pool or a motorhome.

Newborn beluga whales are 5 feet long, which is still very big.

Baby whales have a very strong bond with their mothers. They are in charge of teaching the young how to hunt and navigate the big, wide ocean.

It is important when observing pregnant whales or mothers and their newborns to not disturb them.

In the presence of pregnant orcas, boats are told to stay as far as half a mile away to give them their space to eat comfortably and safely give birth.

Chapter 6 – What's on the Menu?

In this chapter, you will learn what whales eat. Their menu consists of different foods, depending on the type of whale.

A Whale Buffet

A whale's menu changes depending on the whale type. Baleen whales don't have teeth like toothed whales, so they go for smaller meals.

Baleen Whales

Baleen whales, like blue, gray, and humpback whales, use their comb-like teeth to filter food from the ocean. Their mouths open wide to scoop up as much water as possible. They usually catch small creatures this way and spit the water back out.

What They Eat:

- **Small Fish** – herring and anchovies
- **Krill** – shrimp-like creatures
- **Plankton** – tiny little plants and animals that float in the water.

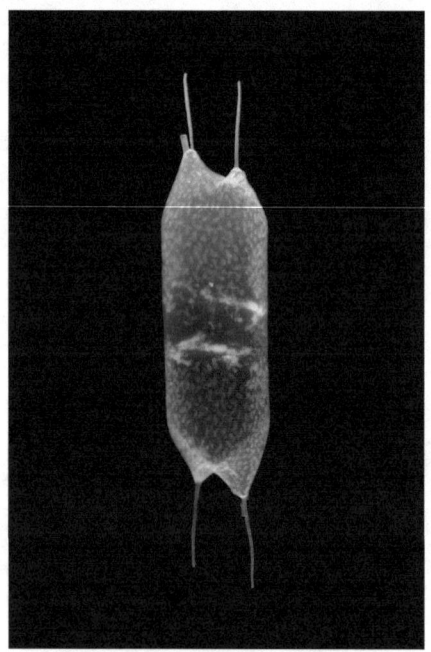

Plankton. Source:
https://commons.wikimedia.org/wiki/File:Marine_plankton_-
_Odontella_sp_(_%3D_Biddulphia_sp)_-
_250x_(14811152768).jpg

Toothed Whales

Toothed whales, such as beluga, sperm, narwhal, and orca, have teeth so they can take large bites of bigger sea animals. Not all toothed-whales go for big fish. Some still enjoy gobbling up tiny food, just like people like to eat little snacks.

What They Eat:

- **Fish** – almost any fish around

- **Octopus** – sperm and pilot whales love an octopus buffet

- **Crabs** – smaller whales and dolphins eat these

- **Squid** – sperm whales love squid the most

- **Seals** – killer whales may hunt seals and other large sea animals

Squid. Source:
https://commons.wikimedia.org/wiki/File:Squid_colors_2.jpg

Baleen Filters Vs. Toothy Bites

Toothed Whales

These smart whale types use sound waves to seek their next meal and find food underwater.

The toothy biters, dolphins, sperm whales, and orcas can use their teeth to hunt down fish, octopus, and other sea creatures when they want a big meal. They can also swallow certain fish and even squids whole!

Baleen Whales

They use their strainer-like mouths to filter water and gather food in the ocean like a sponge.

The crumb catchers, humpback, blue, and gray whales, gulp a huge chunk of water and trap food in, while filtering the water back out like a giant comb. They catch plankton, krill, and other small fish.

The Bubble Net Trick

The bubble net trick is when a whale uses bubbles to make a net. They then use these bubbles to catch fish with the air they breathe out.

Have you ever enjoyed blowing bubbles in your drinks? Well, humpback whales use this trick often to grab their dinner, and it works!

Whales trap fish with teamwork. A pod will dive deep down to the bottom of the ocean to find a school of fish. These are usually small fish like krill and herring.

One of the whales will swim around them in a circle and begin blowing bubbles from their blowhole. As the bubbles rise, they form a circle shape. This frightens the fish and makes them huddle up close together. All the whales then swim over to them and snatch up what they can with one big scoop.

Humpback whales are the only species of whale that does the bubble net trick – and some humpbacks never learn to do it. It's a special skill only used by a few.

Midnight Snackers

Have you ever wanted a snack in the evenings? Well, many whales love to snack around midnight. Whales have many gifts to help them find food to munch on, from senses like sound that help them see in the dark. However, some whales just open their mouths wide and wait for whatever delicious dish gets trapped inside – like a Kinder Surprise!

Day or night, whales can get peckish, but at nighttime specifically, they start to crave yummy underwater snacks. Some whales even take deep dives into the ocean kitchen to see what's on the menu!

After-dark snacks for whales usually include krill, small fish, and plankton. Do you know why whales love these tiny sea creatures? Because some of them glow in the dark! This makes it easier for whales to find and hunt them at night.

Many krill and plankton swim up closer to the surface when it gets dark. This creates a full-on buffet for whales who wait patiently for the parade of treats. Blue whales get very excited about this parade because they mostly eat at night. They also have quite an appetite and are able to eat millions of krill in one meal!

Chapter 7 – Whale Homes and Habitats

Read on to learn all about where whales live and how they adapt to different habitats.

Venture into the homes of the whale! Source: Designed by Freepik. https://www.freepik.com/free-vector/hand-drawn-children-book-illustration_70961885.htm#fromView=search&page=1&position=5 &uuid=e1508e0e-a2df-46db-903b-d4e4ef77152a&query=whale+home

From Arctic to Tropics

Whales can be found in all parts of the ocean. Some whales love the ice-cold areas, while others like to stay in sunny, warm seas. You'll find whales anywhere, from the north and south poles to next to the equator.

Whales don't live in houses – the entire ocean is their home, and they choose an area as their habitat. They choose an area based on what temperatures they like. Just like how some people prefer to live by the beach or in the green countryside, while others love to be in snowy cities. Some whales even travel to and from cold and warm oceans to have babies or find food.

- **Whales in the Arctic**

Some whales love cold places because their skin is thick, so it is easy for them to stay warm. They also prefer the food found in cold climates, like certain fish and seals. These whales include:

1. **Orcas (Killer Whales)** – These whales can live anywhere, and are one of the few whale types that can handle the coldest waters.

2. **Beluga Whales** – These white whales match the snowy areas and love the icy arctic.

3. **Bowhead Whales** – These big-headed whales can break through ice easily, so they stay near the north pole

- **Whales in Comfy, Just-Right Climates**

Some whales are a little like Goldilocks. They like their habitat to be just right – not too cold, not too hot. So, they travel a lot to find what suits their needs. These whales find an ocean in the middle, where they can enjoy water that isn't as cold as the arctic or as warm as the tropical places. Whales that visit or live in these climates include:

1. **Gray Whales** – These can be found swimming the along the coast of alaska to reach hot and sunny Mexico waters.

2. **Humpback Whales** – They love to travel through the middle areas.

- **Whales in the Tropics**

The whales that like warmer habitats find homes in hot, tropical oceans. Baby whales love warm water, so mommy whales travel to these sunny areas to give birth. It's like choosing a cozy vacation home by the beach! Whales that love the heat include:

1. **Bryde's Whales** – These big guys love the heat and prefer to in warm water all year long.

2. **Sperm Whales** – When on the hunt for giant squid, these whales come to the deepest and warmest oceans.

3. **Humpback Whales** – Since humpbacks are travelers, they come to the tropics often, especially in winter when it's time to give birth and raise babies.

Cold Water Champions Vs. Warm Water Wanderers

The cold water champions never get too chilly even though they live near the poles. Their thick skin, or blubber, keeps them warm. The warm water wanderers wander off to the tropical oceans because they love it! They also find these to be the perfect waters to raise their calves.

Here is a list of which whales can withstand the cold and which love the warm weather.

Cold Water Champions

- The strong ice-breaking bowhead
- The Arctic-loving, snow-white beluga
- The twisty-toothed narwhal
- The super intelligent orca

Warm Water Wanderers

- The traveling humpback
- The warm sea-loving, big blue whale
- The squid-eating, deep ocean-loving sperm whale
- The big, warm-water fan, bryde's whale

Deep Ocean Dwellers

Although some whales enjoy exploring near the surface and swimming along the coast, others love a deep dive! The deep ocean dwellers are those who love to dive all the way down to the bottom of the ocean, typically to find dinner.

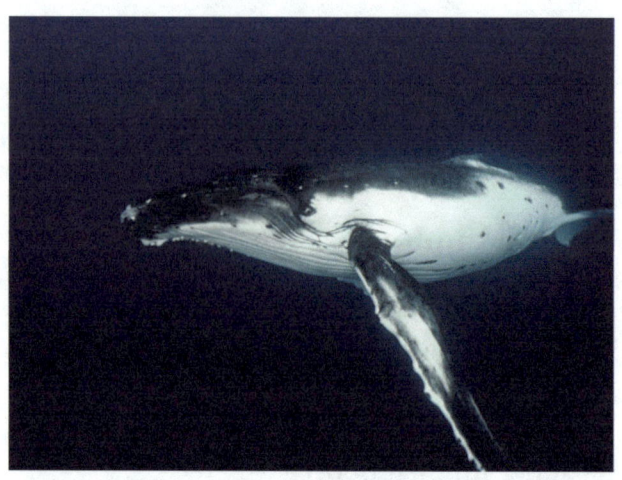

Some whales love a deep sea adventure. Source: https://www.pexels.com/photo/whale-in-blue-depth-of-ocean-4696771/

They have special bodies that help them live comfortably in cold, dark waters. They have tough lungs, so they can hold their breath for hours, large brains to help them navigate the ocean in the dark, and their heartbeats can slow down to hold in air for a long time.

These explorers bravely scout the darkest, coldest, and quietest parts of the underwater world like they're searching for treasure in a big, dark cave.

So, who are these deep ocean whales?

- **Cuvier's Beaked Whale**

They can hold their breath underwater for a whopping 3 hours! It's almost impossible to get these whales up to the surface, so you won't spot them easily in shallow seas. They're quite shy.

- **Blainville's Beaked Whale**

*Source:
https://commons.wikimedia.org/wiki/File:Mesoplodon_densirostr
is.jpg*

Blainville, from the beaked-whale family, is another deep ocean dweller. These giants stay in deep waters because they love hunting squid and other fish that roam the bottom of the sea. Glowing animals can be found in the coldest and darkest parts of the ocean. This makes certain whales choose to live down there, using sound to navigate the area.

- **Sperm Whale**

This deep diver dives the deepest – and goes deeper than most whales. On average, they can dive a mile deep, which is the length of the tallest mountain. These big-brained whales love to be underwater for hours, using sound waves to see in the darkest areas, especially if it means they'll get a giant squid snack!

Coral, Icebergs, and Currents

A whale neighborhood can be surrounded by coral or icebergs with different currents for the whales to ride waves.

For a whale, choosing a neighborhood is like choosing a house. The tropical whales like to be near coral reefs, the cool, arctic whales love the icebergs, and the ocean travelers like to ride the waves of strong currents.

Take a look at these fascinating whale habitats!

Coral Reef

Coral looks like underwater flowers and living rocks. They're colorful and easy to find in tropical areas. It's always warm and sunny by coral reefs, and plenty of fish and other sea creatures live there, too!

It's a favorite hangout for these whales:

- Humpback Whales
- Bryde's Whales

Icebergs

The icy poles have plenty of large, floating icebergs for whales who love taking a cold splash near frozen oceans. The water is very cold, so many seals and penguins live there.

It's a fun, chilly hangout for these whales:

- Beluga Whales
- Bowhead Whales
- Orca Whales

Currents

Ocean currents are a funfair for whales and can even lead them to family. These are the highways where whales swim fast across the ocean. Currents transfer hot and cold water around. This carries food like plankton and krill to different areas and helps whales migrate long distances.

It's a big water park for these whales:

- Humpback Whales
- Gray Whales

Chapter 8 – Whale Trouble and How to Help

Sadly, not everyone treats whales how they should. So, it's important to know how to care for these incredible mammals.

This chapter focuses on troubles whales face and how to help them.

Sadly, some people hunt whales. Source:
https://www.flickr.com/photos/forestservicenw/26159739290

Ocean Dangers

Whales may be big and strong, but everyone needs help from time to time. Here are a few reasons whales need a helping hand to stay safe in the sea.

- **Boats**

Big ships don't always see whales when they swim up to the surface to take a breath. Boats can scare them if they come too close and even hurt them.

How to help:

Boats should slow down when sailing and watch out for whales in the water.

- **Noise**

Whales have very good hearing since they use sound to hunt for food, talk to each other, and navigate long journeys. People and their ships can interfere with what whales need to hear. Oil drilling and other loud noises in or around the water can hurt their ears.

How to help:

Keep whales safe by encouraging quiet zones where they may be swimming.

- **Pollution**

Pollution in the water affects the whales. Source: https://commons.wikimedia.org/wiki/File:Marine_pollution_worl dwide.jpg

Sadly, some people throw waste in the water, not thinking about how fish and mammals can accidentally eat it. Plastic bags, bottles, and balloons can be mistaken for food to a hungry whale, and one can get sick from eating these things.

How to help:

Avoid littering in the ocean, and join recycling and clean-up sessions at the beach to prevent trash from entering the sea.

- **Fishing**

Fishing in areas that aren't suited to it can cause problems for the gentle giants of the sea. Whales can get caught by fishing hooks and gear or tangled in ropes and nets. This can trap and hurt them, making it hard to swim. If they get stuck underwater, they won't be able to come up to breathe.

How to help:

Protect whales by using safe fishing gear and tidying up your nets once you're done.

Whale Hunts: A Sad History

It's important to understand whale history to avoid repeating it. Whales used to face troubles, like whale-hunting for meat, oil, and bones, which hurt them and their families. However, today, many wonderful people are protecting whale families.

People used to hunt whales a long time ago because they didn't have the resources people have today. Whale oil was used to make candles, medicine, and lamps. Whale bones were used to make furniture, toys, and tools. This led to many whales getting hunted, making them almost extinct.

Luckily, whales are no longer needed to make these products and can live happily in the sea.

People began protecting whales because they understood how important they are to the oceans and the planet. Protection laws were made, and safe habitats for whales were left alone, so they could live in peace.

The Whale Rescue Team

There are many heroes who joined the whale rescue team to help whales in trouble. These people are ocean superheroes, like Aquaman, but they wear special clothing and gear to help them go into the water.

The whale rescue team is made up of vets, marine biologists, and people trained to save whales, but many ordinary people volunteer to help, too!

The whale heroes save stranded whales who get stuck on the beach or in shallow waters and need help getting back into the deep ocean. They free whales who got stuck in fishing nets and ropes, and they heal injured whales with medical care so they can go back into the wild healthy.

Be a Whale Protector

Most places have banned whale hunting, but there are many ways to help them continue to live happily.

You, your friends, and family can keep these animals safe by learning about the problems they face, keeping the ocean clean, and sticking to whale-watching to see them instead of disturbing them with loud, noisy boats that could hurt them.

Be their hero by making small changes, such as, avoiding products made from whales and recycling. You can also eat seafood that was caught in a way that doesn't harm whales and plant trees to keep the ocean cool and healthy. These changes will save whale food, too, as krill and fish cannot survive in unhealthy, polluted water.

Bonus Section: Whales Vs Other Ocean Giants

Whales are the giant, gentle mammals of the ocean! The blue whale, especially, is the largest animal on earth, bigger than the largest dinosaur to ever exist.

Other huge sea creatures are sharks, giant sea turtles, colossal and giant squid. Take a look at the differences and similarities between them and your favorite whale friends.

Whale or Shark? (How to Tell Them Apart)

How you can tell the difference between a whale and a shark. Source:
https://upload.wikimedia.org/wikipedia/commons/a/a4/Compari
son_of_size_of_orca_and_great_white_shark.svg

It can be easy to confuse whales and sharks from far away because they're both large and roam the deepest parts of the ocean. However, up close, there are very clear differences. You can tell them apart by looking at their features.

- **Body Type**

Whales – Whales have a smooth, round body like a big tube. They have a wide mouth, and their tail moves up and down to help them swim. They have a blowhole on their heads, and some filter food with baleen, like the blue whale.

Sharks – Sharks have a sleek, pointy body and have gills like other fish on their side of their bodies behind their pectoral fins, so they can breathe underwater. Their tail sways from side to side. They also have very sharp teeth to catch and even tear their prey.

- **Swimming Style**

Whales – Whales use their flippers and flat tail to help them move through the water.
Sharks – Sharks have a dorsal fin on top and fins on their sides. Their tail moves side to side, making them quick and smooth in water.

- **Skin**

Whales – Whales' skin is smooth, and they blend in with the water. Their bellies are a light color and their backs are darker.

Sharks – A shark's skin is rougher with tiny scales, making it feel like sandpaper. They can be brown or grey in color.

Orca (Killer Whale) or Dolphin?

People confuse orcas for dolphins all the time because they look very similar. Check out the few ways to tell them apart!

- **Body Type**

Orcas – Orcas are considered the largest dolphin. They have black and white flesh with a white patch near their eyes. They also have a big dorsal fin on their back and big powerful bodies that can grow as long as a school bus.

Dolphins – Dolphins don't grow to be as big as orcas, and they come in many colors, such as grey, white, and even pink like the amazon river dolphin. Their bodies are sleek, and their dorsal fin is curvy.

- **Taste Buds**

Orcas – Orcas hunt in packs and have a big appetite. They eat everything from fish, seals, to squid, and even other whales.

Dolphins – Dolphins don't have a big palate and stick to eating fish and squid. They don't hunt big prey. They also work together to find food, but rather than hunt fish, they herd them together.

- **Communication and Activity**

Orcas – Orcas live in pods and socialize with their own members. They are loud and powerful when they communicate using calls, clicks, and whistles.

Dolphins – Dolphins are more social and playful. They are very curious and bravely come up to the surface to visit boats full of people. Dolphins also speak with clicks and whistles and play games with others.

- **Homes and Habitats**

Orcas – Orcas can live in cold or warm seas but prefer the deep, cold oceans near the arctic and antarctic.

Dolphins – Dolphins are more tropical. They love to be in warm water near the coast. The bottlenose dolphin, however, is happy to take a dip in cold water from time to time.

Sea Monsters of the Past

There was a time before humans roamed the earth that bigger and stronger creatures lived in the ocean. They are now extinct, but scientists have observed their fossils and have discovered exactly how these enormous sea monsters of the past used to look.

The Giant Lizard, Mosasaurus

Source: https://commons.wikimedia.org/wiki/File:Mosasaurus_hoffmanni _life.jpg

The mosasaurus is a huge sea lizard that lived 65 million years ago, during dinosaur time. It was 50 feet long – the size of an orca.

They would eat fish, reptiles, and even sharks!

The Giant Predator, Pliosaurus

Source: https://commons.wikimedia.org/wiki/File:Pliosaurus_restoration _2019.jpg

150 million years ago, this giant marine reptile, pliosaurus, grew to 40 feet long. It had the sharpest teeth, a powerful jaw, and a massive head.

It was called the top predator because it ate whatever it set its eyes on, even large fish and other reptiles.

Ancient Giant Squids

Source: https://commons.wikimedia.org/wiki/File:Orthocones.jpg

Before the squids we know today existed, there were ancient squid creatures even bigger than the giant squids of today. They lived millions of years ago and were about 100 feet long.

They used to eat fish, crustaceans, and even other squid!

Conclusion

It's been an in-krill-able journey! You've discovered everything there is to know about whales. You've ridden the waves through the stages of a whale's life, such as birth, taking their first breath, and feeding. In each chapter, you explored the different currents that lead to whale paradise. You discovered why whales talk to each other and how they communicate, keep each other company, play games, stay safe, and protect each other. There's a lot to learn from whales, such as how well pods take care of each other. They even eat their meals together after herding krill and squid with teamwork.

You have learned about the two types of whales, baleen and toothed, and how the different species live, find food, play, and even blow air bubbles!

You met the tail dancers, the water surface balancers, and even learned all about whale chatter. You can now tell the difference between whales, dolphins, sharks, and other big fish. You can now name a unique trait of the orca, humpback, and blue whale to impress the fins off your friends!

However, your ocean exploration doesn't have to end here. You can continue to be a whale hero, take up a whale-watching hobby (without disturbing them, of course), teach others about keeping the sea clean, and even try your hand at mimicking whale songs and calls in a fun, karaoke style!

Share your knowledge and help raise awareness about whale safety and other wildlife by protecting the gentle giants of the sea:

1. Avoid littering when on boats

2. Clean up after yourself at the beach

3. Inform others about safe fishing and protecting whale homes and habitats

4. Encourage others to prevent noise pollution, especially when out at sea

Now you have all the information and tools you need to keep up with whale adventures on your own. You can create whale-themed parties and games by making your own quizzes and testing your family and friends' knowledge. Quiz them on the different types of whales, the similarities between tiny giants and other mammal babies, which ones love to sing, and how they hunt for food.

Make a splash by painting and drawing pictures of whale tricks and flips.

You can also find others with an interest in the deep divers and compare the whale facts you've come across. Keep up your curiosity for sea creatures! Who knows, you might become a whale rescuer, a marine biologist, or a vet, and make your mark saving lives under the sea!

Next time you're in the water, try some whale acrobatics! Make a splash, sing, and roll around in the sea.

References

(2025). Twinkl.com.eg. https://www.twinkl.com.eg/blog/what-are-whales-activities-for-kids

AAAS Articles DO Group. (2025). Humpback whale songs are structured like human language. AAAS Articles DO Group. https://doi.org/10.1126/science.znkrt4q

Admin. (2022, August 11). Difference Between Orca and Dolphin. BYJU'S. https://byjus.com/biology/difference-between-orca-and-dolphin/

Afsari, R. (2021, September 21). 5 Ways You Can Save the Whales. Socktopusink. https://socktopusink.com/blogs/news/5-ways-you-can-save-the-whales

Alaska Collection. (2017). Bubble-Net Feeding: Humpback Whales Feeding in Kenai Fjords National Park. Alaskacollection.com. https://www.alaskacollection.com/day-tours/kenai-fjords-tours/stories/what-is-bubble-net-feeding/

Ancient Sea Monster Remains Reveal Oldest Mega-Predatory Pliosaur. (n.d.). ScienceDaily. https://www.sciencedaily.com/releases/2023/10/231020182030.htm

Are, T. (2024). These are the Loudest Animals on Earth. IFAW. https://www.ifaw.org/international/journal/loudest-animals-on-earth

Atwood, A. (2014, January 6). Facts about Whales for Kids. Whale Facts and Information. https://whale-world.com/facts-about-whales-for-kids/

Augliere, B. (2024, August 26). How Humpback Whales Use Bubbles as a Tool. Animals. https://www.nationalgeographic.com/animals/article/humpback-whales-bubbles-tools

Augusta, W. W. (2024, September 16). Whale Birthing and Calf Rearing. Whale Watching Tours Busselton & Augusta | All Sea Charters. https://www.whalewatchingcharters.com.au/whale-birthing-and-calf-rearing/

Bacry, T. C. (2023, March 14). Do Whales Have a Navel? - Baleines en direct. Baleines En Direct. https://baleinesendirect.org/en/les-baleines-ont-elles-un-nombril/

Baldwin, E. (2022, February 16). Orca vs. Dolphin: Main Differences | Ocean Info. Oceaninfo.com. https://oceaninfo.com/compare/orca-vs-dolphin/

Banse, Tom. "Babies on Board! Three Endangered Northwest Killer Whales Look Very Pregnant in Aerial Photos." Northwest News Network, N3, 14 Sept. 2021, www.nwnewsnetwork.org/environment-and-planning/2021-09-14/babies-on-board-three-endangered-northwest-killer-whales-look-very-pregnant-in-aerial-photos. Accessed 16 May 2025.

Better Planet Education. (2024). Whale Hunting. Betterplaneteducation.org.uk. https://betterplaneteducation.org.uk/factsheets/whales-saving-the-whales-whale-hunting

Billington, B. (2024, October 15). Three Islands Whale Shark Dive. Three Islands Whale Shark Dive. https://www.whalesharkdive.com/blog/why-do-humpback-whales-sing/

Blair, J. (2015). Tiny Giants of the Sea – America´s Bilingual Boating Magazine. Yachtingtimesmagazine.com. https://yachtingtimesmagazine.com/2020/01/10/tiny-giants-of-the-sea/

Bluewater Adventures. (2025, May 5). Rubberboot Diaries | Bluewater Adventures. Bluewater Adventures. https://www.bluewateradventures.ca/rubber-boot-diaries/

Boot, T. (2025, January 8). The Emotional Impact of Whale Songs - L-Acoustics The Art of Sound. L-Acoustics the Art of Sound.

https://theartofsound.l-acoustics.com/the-emotional-impact-of-whale-songs/

Bowers, M. (2013, February 12). Day in the Life of a Whale. Tagging Whales in the Antarctic Seas. https://blogs.nicholas.duke.edu/antarctica/day-in-the-life-of-a-whale/

Brearley, L. (2019, June 17). Love Songs for Whale & A Creative Invitation. Community Music Victoria. https://cmvicblog.wordpress.com/2019/06/17/love-songs-for-whales-a-creative-invitation/

Canadian Whale Institute. (n.d.). Campobello Whale Rescue Team. Canadian Whale Institute. https://www.canadianwhaleinstitute.ca/campobello-whale-rescue-team

Captain Bossy Pants. (2024, January 12). The Scenery Changes To Whales and Icebergs | East Antarctica - Sailing Kaihanu. Sailing Kaihanu - Sail the Wild Places. https://sailingkaihanu.com/the-scenery-changes-to-whales-and-icebergs-east-antarctica/

Cheong, E. (2016, September 6). Mini Lesson Plan: Fishes and Whales - LittleLives. Medium; LittleLives. https://blog.littlelives.com/mini-lesson-plan-fishes-and-whales-29520144ffc9

Chivell, L. (2018). 3 Differences Between a Whale and a Shark You Do Not Think About | Hermanus Online Travel Magazine. Hermanusonline.mobi. https://www.hermanusonline.mobi/3-differences-between-a-whale-and-a-shark-you-do-not-think-about

CIMI. (2020, September 5). Blowhole, What are They and What are They Used for? Catalina Island Marine Institute. https://cimi.org/blog/blowhole-what-are-they-and-what-are-they-used-for/

Cormier, Z. (n.d.). The Loudest Voice in the Animal Kingdom | BBC Earth. Www.bbcearth.com. https://www.bbcearth.com/news/the-loudest-voice-in-the-animal-kingdom

Difference between Orca and Dolphin. (2022, August 11). BYJUS; BYJU'S. https://byjus.com/biology/difference-between-orca-and-dolphin/

Dupré, J. (2024, July 25). Are Whales Fish? The MIT Press Reader. https://thereader.mitpress.mit.edu/are-whales-fish/

Fisheries, N. (2021, January 6). Why Do Whales Migrate? They Return to the Tropics to Shed their Skin, Scientists Say | NOAA Fisheries. NOAA. https://www.fisheries.noaa.gov/feature-story/why-do-whales-migrate-they-return-tropics-shed-their-skin-scientists-say

Fisheries, NOAA. "Track Whale Detections with This Interactive Map | NOAA Fisheries." NOAA, 29 June 2022, www.fisheries.noaa.gov/feature-story/track-whale-detections-interactive-map.

Flipse, C. G. (2019, June 16). Humpback Dads. Swim with Whales, Silver Bank Dominican Republic | Conscious Breath Adventures. https://www.consciousbreathadventures.com/blogs/humpback-dads/

Flipse, C. G. (2019, October 6). What Do Humpback Whales Eat? Part 5: Krill. Swim with Whales, Silver Bank Dominican Republic | Conscious Breath Adventures. https://www.consciousbreathadventures.com/blogs/what-do-humpback-whales-eat-part-5-krill/

Florida Atlantic University. "Like Human Societies, Whales Value Culture and Family Ties." EurekAlert!, 5 Apr. 2018, www.eurekalert.org/news-releases/775925. Accessed 16 May 2025.

Forest, A. (2017, November). Minke Whales, from the Arctic to the St. Lawrence to the Tropic of Cancer - Baleines en direct. Baleines En Direct. https://baleinesendirect.org/en/minke-whales-from-the-arctic-to-the-st-lawrence-to-the-tropic-of-cancer/

GeeksforGeeks. (2024, January 17). Difference Between Orca and Dolphin. GeeksforGeeks. https://www.geeksforgeeks.org/difference-between-orca-and-dolphin/

Geer, J. (2024, June 4). The 15 Biggest Deep-Sea Creatures. A-Z Animals. https://a-z-animals.com/animals/lists/biggest-deep-sea-creatures/

Getting to know the Arctic's whales - WWF Arctic. (2024, July 10). WWF Arctic. https://www.arcticwwf.org/the-circle/stories/getting-to-know-the-arctics-whales/

Giants, T. (2025). Tiny Giants. Tiny Giants. https://www.tinygiantsclothing.com/vintage-surf/n444in5upqbysw1xh3s8rz5dc9pub0-6s7bp

Giles, A. (2025, March 26). 4,000 Tons of Nitrogen and 20 Million Big Macs: What Whales Bring to the Tropics Every Year in Nutrients. Maine Public; WMEH. https://www.mainepublic.org/2025-03-26/4000-tons-

20-million-big-macs-whales-bring-tropics-nutrients-nitrogen-phosphorus-whale-pee

Gupta, Arpana. "Did You Know... Whales Experience Joy, Grief and Empathy?" Medium, Did You Know...Short Fun Facts, 4 May 2025, medium.com/did-you-know-short-fun-facts/did-you-know-whales-experience-joy-grief-and-empathy-fd87bcbdcc57. Accessed 16 May 2025.

Harbor Breeze. (2019, May 23). Do Whales Give Birth or Lay Eggs? Harbor Breeze Cruises. https://2seewhales.com/blog/how-do-whales-give-birth/

Henry, L. (2010). Whale | Species | WWF. World Wildlife Fund. https://www.worldwildlife.org/species/whale

History of Whaling | Hull History Centre. (n.d.). Www.hullhistorycentre.org.uk. https://www.hullhistorycentre.org.uk/research/research-guides/whaling-history.aspx

Holly. (2020, February 22). Midnight Snacks | Bluewater Adventures. Bluewater Adventures. https://www.bluewateradventures.ca/rubber-boot-diaries/midnight-snacks/

How Big Are Baby Whales? | Book a Whale & Dolphin Safari. (n.d.). Capt. Dave's Dolphin & Whale Watching Safari. https://www.dolphinsafari.com/how-big-are-baby-whales/

How Do Whales Communicate? (2023, March 5). BBC Newsround. https://www.bbc.co.uk/newsround/64846776

How Whales Stay Warm - New Bedford Whaling Museum. (n.d.). Www.whalingmuseum.org. https://www.whalingmuseum.org/classroom-tool/how-whales-stay-warm/

Inicio. (2020). Panda.org. https://wwf.panda.org/es/

Kelly, K. (2025, March 3). Whales, Coral Reefs, and the Future of Our Oceans - Coral Reef Alliance. Coral Reef Alliance. https://coral.org/en/blog/whales-coral-reefs-and-the-future-of-our-oceans/

Kelly, Nat. "The Surprising Intelligence of Whales." MDPI Blog, 8 Nov. 2023, blog.mdpi.com/2023/11/08/surprising-intelligence-of-whales/.

Kiefer, P. (2021, November 3). Biologists Vastly Underestimated How Much Whales Eat and Poop. Popular Science. https://www.popsci.com/science/biologists-underestimated-whales-poop/

Kommana, Y. (2021). How Humpback Whales Communicate Through a Hidden Global Network of Song. Sciencefocus.com. https://www.sciencefocus.com/nature/whale-song

Krynen, Jos . "What Are Baby Orcas Called? Everything You Need to Know." Eagleeyeadventures.com, 2024, www.eagleeyeadventures.com/blog/what-are-baby-orcas-called-everything-you-need-to-know.

Krynen, Jos. "Whale Wise Rules." Eagleeyeadventures.com, 2021, www.eagleeyeadventures.com/blog/whale-wise-rules. Accessed 16 May 2025.

Lambert, J. (2021, December 1). Baleen Whales Eat — and Poop — A lot More than We Thought. Science News Explores. https://www.snexplores.org/article/baleen-whales-eat-poop-more-food-ecosystem

Large Whales and Vessel Strikes - Marine Mammal Commission. (2024, December 6). Marine Mammal Commission. https://www.mmc.gov/priority-topics/vessel-strikes

Lindsey, M. (2015, June 30). Marta Lindsey, Children's Author. Marta Lindsey, Children's Author. https://www.martalindsey.com/blogs-all/2015/6/30/top-three-ways-kids-and-everyone-can-help-gray-whales-and-our-oceans

Livermore, S. (2020, June 2). Five of the Big Threats to Life in Our Oceans. IFAW. https://www.ifaw.org/eu/journal/five-biggest-threats-to-ocean

Longrich, N. R. (n.d.). "Sea monsters" Were Real Millions of Years Ago. New Fossils Tell About Their Rise and Fall. The Conversation. https://theconversation.com/sea-monsters-were-real-millions-of-years-ago-new-fossils-tell-about-their-rise-and-fall-191089

Lotzof, K. (2017). Life in the Pod: The Social Lives of Whales | Natural History Museum. Nhm.ac.uk. https://www.nhm.ac.uk/discover/social-lives-of-whales

Mammal, M. (2017, March 15). A Sad History of Whaling. International Marine Mammal Project. https://savedolphins.eii.org/news/a-sad-history-of-whaling

Marine Animal Rescue and Response - Whale & Dolphin Conservation USA. (2021). Whales.org. https://us.whales.org/whales-dolphins/science/marine-animal-rescue-and-response/

Mathew, Naomi. "The Award for the Largest Brain in the World Goes To..." Whale Scientists, 3 Feb. 2023, whalescientists.com/the-award-for-the-largest-brain-in-the-world-goes-to/.

National Geographic. (2017, January 5). Threats Facing The Oceans and Their Species. National Geographic. https://www.nationalgeographic.com/environment/article/ocean-threats

NCCOS. (n.d.). How do Ocean Currents Connect Coral Reefs among Islands in the Mariana Archipelago, and How will Climate Change Affect Them? NCCOS Coastal Science Website. https://coastalscience.noaa.gov/project/ocean-currents-connect-coral-reefs/

Next Level Sailing. "Your Complete Guide to Baby Whales - Guide to Understanding Baby Whales." Next Level Sailing, 22 July 2022, nextlevelsailing.com/your-complete-guide-to-baby-whales/.

Novak, Sara. "Sperm Whales Have the Biggest Brains, but How Smart Are They?" Discover Magazine, 19 Nov. 2022, www.discovermagazine.com/planet-earth/sperm-whales-have-the-biggest-brains-but-how-smart-are-they.

Ocean Portal Team. "Whales and Dolphins." Smithsonian Ocean, 25 Nov. 2024, www.ocean.si.edu/ocean-life/marine-mammals/whales.

Osterloff, E. (n.d.). What do Whales Eat for Dinner? Www.nhm.ac.uk. https://www.nhm.ac.uk/discover/what-do-whales-eat-for-dinner.html

Partnerships for Reform through Investigative Science and Math. (n.d.). https://hilo.hawaii.edu/affiliates/prism/documents/Howdowhalesstaywarm.pdf

Philips, Charlie. "How Intelligent Are Whales and Dolphins? - Whale and Dolphin Conservation." Whale & Dolphin Conservation UK, uk.whales.org/whales-dolphins/how-intelligent-are-whales-and-dolphins/.

Picher-Labrie, Jeanne. "How Do Whales Show Their Emotions?" Baleines En Direct, 13 May 2021, baleinesendirect.org/en/how-do-whales-show-their-emotions/.

published, C. M. (2024, June 3). 32 of the Loudest Animals on Earth. Livescience.com. https://www.livescience.com/animals/32-of-the-loudest-animals-on-earth

published, P. P. (2023, April 10). 25 of the Strangest Ancient Sea Monsters. Livescience.com. https://www.livescience.com/strangest-ancient-sea-monsters

Rahaim, N. (2022, March 11). Whales and Fishers Compete for What's on the Line. High Country News. https://www.hcn.org/articles/wildlife-whales-and-fishers-compete-for-whats-on-the-line/

Reilly, J. (2017, February 28). Do Whales Like it Hot? - ICWA. Institute of Current World Affairs. https://www.icwa.org/do-whales-like-it-hot/

Roper, C. (2019, June 24). Giant Squid. Smithsonian Ocean. https://ocean.si.edu/ocean-life/invertebrates/giant-squid

S., C. (2024, December 27). Welcome to the Whale Fall Buffet! Athena's Advanced Academy. https://athenasacademy.com/scientific-contributions-welcome-to-the-whale-fall-buffet/

Sailors for the Sea. (2024, January 23). Tiny Giants of the Sea. Sailors for the Sea. https://sailorsforthesea.org/ocean-watch-essays/tiny-giants-sea/

Sea Goddess Whale Watching. (2020, March 20). Sea Goddess Whale Watching. https://seagoddesswhalewatch.com/blog/seasonal-ocean-travelers-in-the-monterey-bay/

Shape of Life. (n.d.). Whale Communication | Shape of Life. Www.shapeoflife.org. https://www.shapeoflife.org/blog/whale-communication

Shark and Whale Showdown | God's World News. (2017, August 30). Kids.gwnews.com. https://kids.gwnews.com/articles/shark-and-whale-showdown

Shark vs. Whale - What's the Difference? | This vs. That. (2023). This vs. That. https://thisvsthat.io/shark-vs-whale

Sigwart, M. (2023, September 14). Speaking, Singing, and Clicking in Whale | Datawrapper Blog. Datawrapper. https://blog.datawrapper.de/whale-sounds-map/

Speaking, Singing, and Clicking in Hale | Datawrapper Blog. (2023, September 14). Datawrapper. https://www.datawrapper.de/blog/whale-sounds-map

Tudor Vieru. (2013, November). Softpedia. https://news.softpedia.com/news/Humpback-Whales-Enjoy-Midnight-Snacks-as-Much-as-Anyone-396251.shtml

University of Queensland. (2023, February 16). Whales Give Up SInging to Fight for Love. Phys.org. https://phys.org/news/2023-02-whales.html

US Department of Commerce, N. O. and A. A. (n.d.). Ten Dangers at the Beach. Oceanservice.noaa.gov. https://oceanservice.noaa.gov/hazards/beach-dangers/

US Department of Commerce, National Oceanic and Atmospheric Administration. (2019). Why do whales make sounds? Noaa.gov. https://oceanservice.noaa.gov/facts/whalesounds.html

Webmaster. "Science behind Whale Migration: An In-Depth Look for Enthusiasts." Australiawhaleexperience.com.au, 29 Oct. 2023, australiawhaleexperience.com.au/science-behind-whale-migration-an-in-depth-look-for-enthusiasts/.

Weiler, C. (2022, February 23). Is an orca (killer whale) a whale or a dolphin? Whale & Dolphin Conservation USA. https://us.whales.org/2022/02/23/is-an-orca-killer-whale-a-whale-or-a-dolphin/

Whale and Dolphin Record Breakers - Whale and Dolphin Conservation. (n.d.). Whale & Dolphin Conservation UK. https://uk.whales.org/whales-dolphins/record-breakers/

Whale Communication | Shape of Life. (n.d.). Www.shapeoflife.org. https://www.shapeoflife.org/blog/whale-communication

Whale Facts for Kids - Twinkl Homework Help - Twinkl. (2025). Twinkl. https://www.twinkl.com.eg/homework-help/geography-homework-help/continents-and-oceans/whale-facts-for-kids

Whale Facts. (2012, January 20). Do Whales Have Belly Buttons? Whale Facts. https://www.whalefacts.org/do-whales-have-belly-buttons/

Whale Migration: Patterns, Currents, and Communication. (2025, April 30). BiologyInsights. https://biologyinsights.com/whale-migration-patterns-currents-and-communication/

Whale Records: Faster, Bigger, Longer-lived • Renewables. (2025, February 24). Renovables. https://renovables.blog/en/zoologia/los-records-de-las-ballenas-mas-rapidas-mas-grandes-mas-longevas/

Whale Sizes: Largest To Smallest - List Of Whale Species According To Size - How Big Is A Whale, Largest To Smallest. (n.d.). Next Level Sailing. https://nextlevelsailing.com/how-big-is-a-whale-list-of-whales-by-size/

Whale-Watching Guidelines Don't Include Boat Noise. It's Time They Did. (2023). Uwa.edu.au. https://www.uwa.edu.au/news/article/2023/april/whale-watching-guidelines-dont-include-boat-noise-its-time-they-did

Whales - Meet the Different Species - Whale and Dolphin Conservation. (n.d.). Whale & Dolphin Conservation UK. https://uk.whales.org/whales-dolphins/whales/

Whales Online. (n.d.). Mother-Calf Relationships. Baleines En Direct. https://baleinesendirect.org/en/discover/life-of-whales/behaviour/mother-calf-relationships/

Whales, P. of. (2023, July 6). What Do Whales Eat? Prince of Whales. https://princeofwhales.com/what-do-whales-eat/

Whale's Tail Charters | Gray Whale Calves | Learn More. (2024, July 5). Whales Tail Charters. https://whalestaildepoebay.com/gray-whale-calves/

Wharf, D. (2024, August 2). The Diet of Whales: What Do The Giants of the Ocean Eat. Dana Wharf. https://danawharf.com/blog/8372/

Wharf, D. (2024, August 26). The Lives of Baby Whales. Dana Wharf. https://danawharf.com/blog/8409/

Wharf, D. (2025). Anatomy of Whale Birth: A Deep Dive into Cetacean Reproduction. Dana Wharf. https://danawharf.com/blog/the-fascinating-process-of-whale-birth/

Wharf, D. (2025, January 7). Understanding Whale Communication: Sounds and Signals. Dana Wharf.

https://danawharf.com/blog/understanding-whale-communication-sounds-and-signals/

Wharf, D. "The Lives of Baby Whales." Dana Wharf, 26 Aug. 2024, danawharf.com/blog/8409/.

What Is the Difference Between a Whale and a Whale Shark? - Seafood Peddler. (2023, August 10). Seafood Peddler. https://www.seafoodpeddler.com/what-difference-between-whale-whale-shark/

Williams, A. (2011, June 28). Killer Bubbles: Humpback Whales Use Bubble-nets to Capture Prey. Audubon. https://www.audubon.org/news/killer-bubbles-humpback-whales-use-bubble-nets-capture-prey

WWF Protecting Whales & Dolphins Initiative. (n.d.). WWF Protecting Whales & Dolphins Initiative. https://wwfwhales.org/

WWF. (n.d.). Meet the Biggest Animal in the World. World Wildlife Fund. https://www.worldwildlife.org/stories/meet-the-biggest-animal-in-the-world

"Guidelines for Respectful Whale Watching." Firmm.org, 2025, www.firmm.org/en/whale-watching/respectful. Accessed 16 May 2025.

"Know When to Slow down for Whales." Gard, Gard AS, 27 Nov. 2024, gard.no/insights/know-when-to-slow-down-for-whales/. Accessed 16 May 2025.

"Whale & Dolphin Tracker Live Sightings Map | PWF." Pacific Whale Foundation, 14 Mar. 2024, www.pacificwhale.org/what-we-do/research/learn-about-marine-life/whale-dolphin-tracker-live-sightins-map/.

"Whale Trail Viewing Guide." The Whale Trail, 26 Mar. 2018, thewhaletrail.org/dive-deeper/whale-trail-viewing-guide/.

Made in United States
Cleveland, OH
17 July 2025

18607839R00050